Mark Sanchez

By Jeff Savage

AMAZING ATHLETES

⌊ Lerner Publications Company • Minneapolis

Lerner Publications Company
A division of Lerner Publishing Group, Inc.
241 First Avenue North
Minneapolis, MN 55401 U.S.A.

Website address: www.lernerbooks.com

Library of Congress Cataloging-in-Publication Data

Savage, Jeff, 1961–
    Mark Sanchez / by Jeff Savage.
        p.   cm. — (Amazing athletes)
    Includes index.
    ISBN 978–0–7613–7673–6 (lib. bdg. : alk. paper)
    1. Sanchez, Mark—Juvenile literature. 2. Football players—United States—Biography—Juvenile literature. 3. Quarterbacks (Football)—United States—Biography—Juvenile literature. 4. Hispanic American football players—Biography—Juvenile literature. I. Title.
GV939.S175S28 2012
796.332092—dc22 [B]   2011004332

Manufactured in the United States of America
1 – BP – 7/15/11

TABLE OF CONTENTS

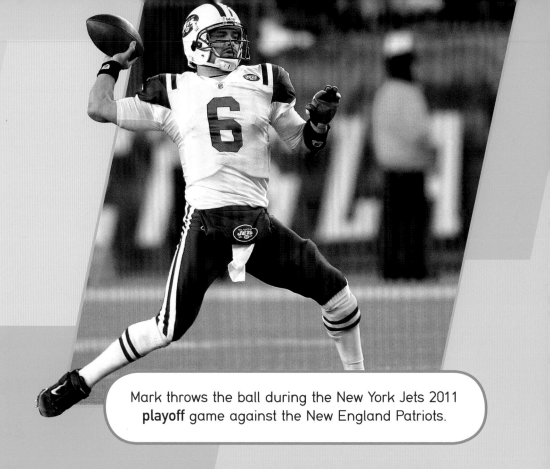

Mark throws the ball during the New York Jets 2011 **playoff** game against the New England Patriots.

BIG WIN

New York Jets **quarterback** Mark Sanchez looked down the field. New England Patriots **defenders** swarmed around him. Mark scooted left to escape the rush. He pointed for **wide receiver** Braylon Edwards to run deep. Mark launched the football far down the left side of the field. Edwards caught the pass for a 37–yard gain. Two plays later, Mark fired a strike to LaDainian Tomlinson for a **touchdown**. Mark's Jets were in the lead, 7–3.

Few people thought the Jets could win this 2011 playoff game. The Patriots had the best record in the National Football League (NFL). They were playing on their home field. A month earlier, the Jets had lost to the Patriots, 42–3.

Patriots fans at Gillette Stadium were fired up for the big game.

Mark is serious on the field. Off it, he likes to have fun. "He can be goofy," says former Jets player Kris Jenkins. "He's one of those California surfer-type dudes."

Mark had led the Jets to victory over the Indianapolis Colts a week earlier. He felt confident. But Mark was also just 24 years old. Most people didn't think he would play well against the tough New England defenders.

The Jets had the ball again. Tomlinson ran for 16 yards. Then he ran for six more. On the next play, Mark zipped the ball to Edwards across the middle. The wide receiver sprinted into the **end zone**. The crowd was stunned. The Jets led the game, 14–3.

Patriots quarterback Tom Brady brought his team back. He led New England on an 80-yard drive for a touchdown. A **two-point conversion** cut the Jets' lead to 14–11.

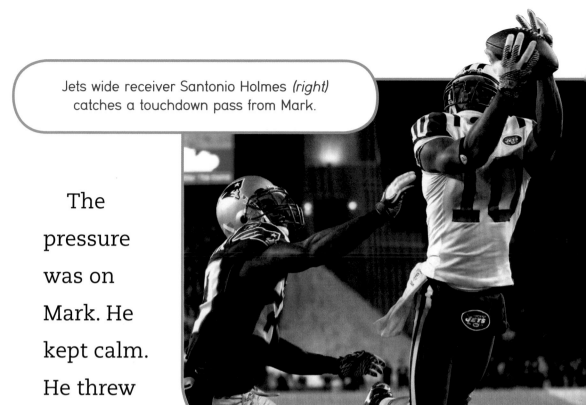

Jets wide receiver Santonio Holmes *(right)* catches a touchdown pass from Mark.

The pressure was on Mark. He kept calm. He threw to Dustin Keller for seven yards. He hit Jerricho Cotchery who sprinted for 58 yards. The Jets needed seven more yards for another touchdown. Mark threw a perfect pass to the left corner of the end zone. Santonio Holmes caught the ball for the score. Edwards called the pass "maybe [Mark's] best throw of the season."

The Patriots kicked a **field goal** to make the score 21–14 with two minutes left in the game. Both teams scored again, but New England could not catch up. The Jets shocked the Patriots, 28–21. New York needed just one more win to reach the Super Bowl.

Mark celebrates with fans after the Jets victory.

Long Beach is in Southern California, near Los Angeles.

YOUNG LEADER

Mark Sanchez was born November 11, 1986, in Long Beach, California. He grew up in nearby Rancho Santa Margarita. Mark's parents, Nick and Olga, divorced when Mark was four. Nick later married a woman named Maddy. Together they raised Mark and his two older brothers, Nick and Brandon. Olga stayed in her sons' lives by taking three-hour bus rides to see them.

Mark and his brothers were taught to be confident. When meeting a new person, the boys introduced themselves first. They were first in line at school and first to give a report in front of the class. When Mark's father dropped the boys off for school each morning, he told them: "Be a leader today."

Mark understands why his parents raised them this way. "Now when I have to be the center of attention, I'm comfortable," says Mark. "I've been doing it all my life."

Mark had to earn at least a B+ in all his subjects to be allowed to play sports. His father taught him to focus. As Mark shot free throws, he had to spell words. As he hit baseballs in the batting cage, he had to solve math problems. Mark liked the challenge.

Mark was tall for his age. When he was

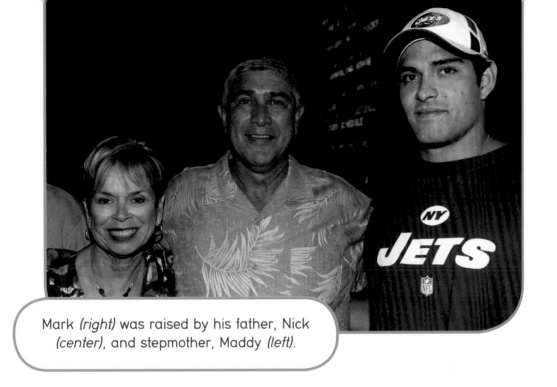

Mark *(right)* was raised by his father, Nick *(center)*, and stepmother, Maddy *(left)*.

10 years old, he stood five feet, nine inches. In 1998, at the age of 12, Mark became the quarterback on his football team. Mark's father had been a quarterback in high school. Mark's oldest brother, Nick, played quarterback at Yale University.

Mark played football at Rancho Santa Margarita High School. His first pass as a sophomore went for 55 yards and the game-winning touchdown.

Mark changed schools before his junior year. He decided to go to Mission Viejo High School. The football coach at Mission Viejo was Bob Johnson. Coach Johnson was an experienced football coach. He had helped his son Rob thrive at the University of Southern California (USC) and in the NFL. Mark knew he could learn a lot from Coach Johnson.

As a junior in 2004, Mark

Mark looks for a receiver while playing for Mission Viejo High School.

completed over 75 percent of his passes. He threw for almost 2,500 yards and 29 touchdowns. As a senior, he tossed 24 touchdown passes to lead Mission Viejo to the state title.

Mark's two-year record at Mission Viejo was 27–1. He was considered among the best high school players in the country. Top college football programs wanted him. He turned down offers from Ohio State University and the University of Notre Dame. There was only one choice for Mark—USC and Coach Pete Carroll.

Mark's idol was Cincinnati Bengal's quarterback Carson Palmer. Palmer also grew up in California and played quarterback at USC. One day, when Mark was 13, he got to go into USC's locker room. The equipment manager gave him some wristbands with the USC colors.

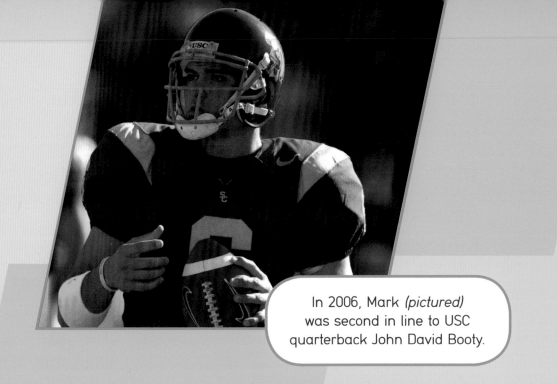

In 2006, Mark *(pictured)* was second in line to USC quarterback John David Booty.

TROJAN HERO

The USC Trojans were a football power. The team was filled with good players. Mark played quarterback on the practice team as a freshman. He still had a lot to learn.

As a **redshirt freshman** in 2006, Mark was the backup to John David Booty. Mark threw only seven passes during games all year. As a sophomore, he was named backup again. But midway through the 2007 season, Booty broke his finger. Mark was thrust into the starting role.

Mark's first game as a starter was against the University of Arizona. He was nervous. He threw two **interceptions** in the first half. Coach Carroll helped calm him down. Mark fired a touchdown pass in the second half to lead USC to a 20–13 win.

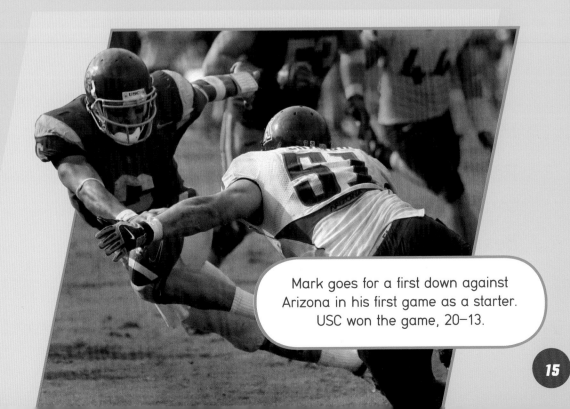

Mark goes for a first down against Arizona in his first game as a starter. USC won the game, 20–13.

Trojans coach Pete Carroll *(left)* shakes Mark's hand before a game.

The following week, the Trojans faced the tough Notre Dame Fighting Irish on the road. Mark knew he would have to play better.

The game was shown on national television. Mark was brilliant. He completed 21 of 38 passes for 235 yards. He also threw four touchdowns with no interceptions. The Trojans beat the Irish by their biggest margin ever, 38–0. One game later, Booty returned to the lineup. Mark went back to the bench.

After the season, Mark worked as a cook in a restaurant. He focused on his studies. He prepared hard for his junior year. Booty had moved on to the NFL. That meant Mark would be the starting quarterback at USC.

Mark is proud of his Latino background. When at USC, he visited schools with mostly Hispanic students. He joined the mayor of Los Angeles in passing out gifts to needy families. He took Spanish classes so he could do interviews with the Spanish-language media without a translator.

But one day at practice, he fell awkwardly. "I looked down," he said, "and my kneecap was on the wrong side of my leg." Mark had suffered a serious knee injury. He wanted to practice the next day. Doctors made him sit for two weeks.

Mark's knee was healed and ready for the first game of the 2008 season.

Mark gets hit by an Ohio State defender after throwing a pass. Mark threw four touchdown passes in this game.

He carved up the Virginia Cavaliers with 338 yards passing. Mark also threw three touchdowns in a 52–7 victory.

The Trojans were ranked number one in the **polls**. To stay in front, they would need to win all their games. The following week, they crushed Ohio State, 35–3. Mark threw four touchdown passes. "He's a resourceful quarterback," Coach Carroll said.

The next week at Oregon State, the Trojans were shocked in a 27–21 loss. USC's dreams of winning a national title were shattered.

The Trojans won the rest of their games in 2008. Mark threw 34 touchdown passes. This was the second most in school history. In the Rose Bowl against Penn State University, Mark passed for 413 yards in a 34–24 win. He was named the game's Most Valuable Player (MVP).

Two weeks later, Mark announced that he would skip his senior year at USC. He was about to complete his studies in communications. Mark declared that he would enter the 2009 NFL **draft**.

Mark celebrates after winning the Rose Bowl against Penn State.

Mark *(wearing hat)* holds up his new Jets jersey after being selected in the NFL draft. Next to him is his family, including his mother, Olga Macias *(holding jersey)*.

SANCHISE

The New York Jets wanted Mark. They used the fifth pick of the 2009 NFL draft to get him. The Jets offered Mark a five-year **contract** worth $50 million. This was the largest contract in team history. Mark was named the team's starting quarterback.

New York is the biggest U.S. city. The city's fans expect a lot. But Mark never wavered. His boyhood lessons in confidence were about to pay off.

In his first game, Mark passed for 272 yards and a touchdown. The Jets beat the Houston Texans, 24–7. Mark was named NFL Rookie of the Week.

During his rookie season, New York fans gave Mark the nickname Sanchise. Sanchise is a combination of the words *Sanchez* and *franchise*.

Mark throws a touchdown pass against the Houston Texans in his first NFL game.

A week later, in the team's first home game, Mark led the Jets to a 16–9 victory over the New England Patriots.

The Jets next beat the Tennessee Titans, 24–17. Mark became the first rookie quarterback to win his first three games. Said teammate Kerry Rhodes: "I honestly don't think this kid knows he's the quarterback of a New York football team. He's so cool."

Mark celebrates with teammates after completing a touchdown pass against the Titans.

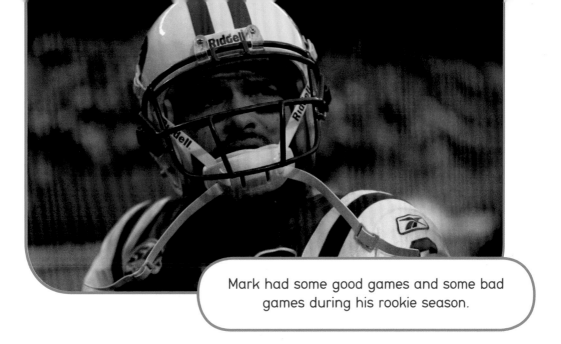

Mark had some good games and some bad games during his rookie season.

The high-flying Jets suddenly ran into trouble. Against the New Orleans Saints, Mark did not play well. The Jets lost, 24–10. Then they lost again, 31–27, to the Miami Dolphins. They lost their third straight game to the Buffalo Bills, 16–13. Mark threw five interceptions in the game. Mark was upset after the loss to Buffalo. "I am embarrassed," he said. "It was totally my fault."

The Jets won enough games to sneak into the playoffs. Then they caught fire. They beat the Cincinnati Bengals, 24–14.

Mark was good, completing 12 of 15 passes for 182 yards and a touchdown. Then the Jets stunned the Chargers in San Diego, 17–14. Mark became just the second rookie quarterback to win two playoff games.

Next was the **American Football Conference (AFC) Championship Game** at Indianapolis. Mark connected with Edwards on an 80-yard bomb. The Jets led the Colts 17–13 at halftime. If they could hold on to the lead, the Jets would be in the Super Bowl! But quarterback Peyton Manning and the Colts could not be stopped in the second half. The Jets lost, 30–17.

Colts quarterback Peyton Manning makes a pass during the AFC Championship Game against the Jets.

Mark greets Jets fans during training camp in 2010.

HIGH-FLYING JET

Mark was eager to begin the 2010 season. He spent long days studying game film with former quarterback Rich Gannon. He studied the Jets game plan. When training camp opened, he felt ready to go. "Play-calls just roll off my tongue," said Mark. "I'm speaking the language. It helps our chemistry on offense."

The Jets reached the playoffs again. Their first game was at Indianapolis. The Colts had a two-point lead with 53 seconds to go. Would Indianapolis knock New York out of the playoffs for the second year in a row?

Sanchez and the Jets did not give up. They marched down the field. Mark's 18–yard pass to Edwards moved the ball to the Colts' 14-yard line. Just three seconds were left in the game. Nick Folk drilled a field goal. The Jets won, 17–16.

The next week, the Jets shocked the Patriots. New York would play in the AFC

Mark talks with Jets coach Rex Ryan (right) before the AFC Championship Game against the Steelers.

championship game for the second year in a row. Coach Rex Ryan was impressed with his young quarterback. "This guy is more confident than I am, which is saying something," the coach said.

New York's Super Bowl hopes were spoiled the next week in Pittsburgh.

The Steelers jumped out to a 24–0 lead. Mark brought his team back in the second half. He threw touchdown passes to Holmes and Cotchery. New York cut the lead to 24–19 with three minutes left. But that was as close as the Jets would get. "I came up short," Mark said. "But I was proud of our guys. We almost came back."

> The Jets barely missed playing in the 2011 Super Bowl. Mark went anyway. He helped raise $25,000 for an organization that helps kids suffering with diabetes.

Mark is a winner. He won in high school and college. He won during his first two seasons with the Jets. He plans to keep on winning. "We want to get to the Super Bowl, and we need a quarterback who can get us there," Mark says. "I believe I am that quarterback. I think I have a natural ability to lead. It's a joy to do it here in New York. It's the best feeling in the world to know you're the guy they're counting on. I'm proud to be that guy."

Mark is proud to know his teammates and fans are counting on him to lead the Jets to victory.

Selected Career Highlights

2010–2011 Led Jets to two playoff road victories and the AFC Championship Game
Tied the NFL all-time quarterback record for most road wins in playoff history

2009–2010 Led Jets to two playoff road victories and AFC Championship Game
Became the second rookie quarterback in NFL history to win two playoff games
Named NFL Rookie of the Week three times
Set Jets record for most passing yards (2,444) by a rookie
Became the first rookie quarterback in NFL history to win his first three games

2008 Led USC to Rose Bowl victory
Named Rose Bowl MVP
Threw 34 touchdown passes, second most in USC history
Led USC to the number one ranking early in the season
Led USC to a 12–1 record

2007 Led USC to a 38–0 win over Notre Dame—the largest margin ever between the teams

2006 Completed 3 of 7 passes as a redshirt freshman

2005 Led scout team in practice

2004 Named *Parade* All-America Player of the Year
Named Super Prep All-America Player of the Year
Named Gatorade California Player of the Year
Led Mission Viejo High to the state title

2003 Completed more than 75 percent of passes for nearly 2,500 yards and 29 touchdowns

2002 Completed first varsity pass for a game-winning touchdown

Glossary

American Football Conference (AFC) Championship Game: a playoff game in which the two top teams in the American Football Conference play to decide who will go to the Super Bowl

contract: a deal signed by a player and a team that states the amount of money the player is paid and the number of years the player will play

defenders: players whose job it is to stop the other team from scoring points

draft: a yearly event in which teams take turns choosing new players from a group

end zone: the area beyond the goal line at the end of a football field. A team scores six points when it reaches the other team's end zone.

field goal: a successful kick over the U-shaped upright poles. A field goal is worth three points.

franchise: in sports, the player most valuable to a team and its future

interceptions: passes caught by the defense. Interceptions result in the opposing team getting control of the ball.

playoff: one of a series of games held every year to decide a championship

polls: lists made by coaches and media members that rank college football teams. The best team in the country is ranked number one.

quarterback: a player whose main job is to lead the offense

redshirt freshman: a second-year freshman. The player is given this extra year because the previous season the player was allowed to practice with the team and wear a uniform for the game but was not permitted to play.

touchdown: a six-point score. A team scores a touchdown when it gets into the other team's end zone with the ball.

two-point conversion: a scoring play made immediately after a touchdown that is worth two points. A team can get the two points by running or passing the ball into the opponent's end zone on one play starting from the opponent's two-yard line.

wide receiver: a player who catches passes

Further Reading & Websites

Kennedy, Mike, and Mark Stewart. *Touchdown: The Power and Precision of Football's Perfect Play*. Minneapolis: Millbrook Press, 2010.

Savage, Jeff. *Peyton Manning*. Minneapolis: Lerner Publications Company, 2008.

Savage, Jeff. *Tom Brady*. Minneapolis: Lerner Publications Company, 2009.

Williams, Zella. *Mark Sanchez: Quarterback on the Rise*. New York: PowerKids Press, 2011.

New York Jets: The Official Site
http://www.jets.com
The official website of the New York Jets includes the team schedule and game results, late-breaking news, biographies of players like Mark Sanchez, and much more.

Sports Illustrated Kids
http://www.sikids.com
The *Sports Illustrated Kids* website covers all sports, including football.

Index

Photo Acknowledgments

The images in this book are used with the permission of: AP Photo/
Stephan Savoia, p. 4; AP Photo/David Drapkin, pp. 5, 25; © Andrew Mills/The
Star-Ledger via US Presswire, p. 7; AP Photo/Charles Krupa, p. 8; © Robert
Harding Picture Library/SuperStock, p. 9; AP Photo/Hector Mata, p. 11;
© Marin Media/Cal Sport Media/ZUMA Press, p. 12; © John Pyle/Cal Sport
Media/ZUMA Press, p. 14; © Hans Gutknecht/LA Daily News/ZUMA Press,
p. 15; AP Photo/Ted S. Warren, p. 16; AP Photo/Mark Avery, p. 18; AP Photo/
Mark J. Terrill, p. 19; © James Lang/US Presswire, p. 20; AP Photo/David J.
Phillip, p. 21; AP Photo/Tim Larsen, p. 22; AP Photo/Seth Wenig, p. 23; AP
Photo/Paul Spinelli, p. 24; © Joe Robbins/Getty Images, p. 26; AP Photo/Bill
Kostroun, p. 28; © Rob Tringali/SportsChrome/Getty Images, p. 29.

Front cover: © Andrew Burton/Getty Images.

Main body text set in Caecilia LT std 55 Roman 16/28. Typeface provided by
Linotype AG.